READING POWER

Famous American Trails

The Overland Trail

From Atchison, Kansas, to Ft. Bridger, Wyoming

Arlan Dean

The Rosen Publishing Group's
PowerKids Press™
New York

Published in 2003 by The Rosen Publishing Group, Inc.
29 East 21st Street, New York, NY 10010

First Edition

Book Design: Christopher Logan

Photo Credits: Cover, Wells Fargo History Museum; pp. 4–5, 15 (inset) Milstein Division of Local History, United States History and Genealogy, The New York Public Library, Astor, Lenox and Tilden Foundations; p. 5 (inset) Christopher Logan; pp. 6–7, 14–15, 17 © Hulton/Archive/Getty Images; p. 6 (inset) © Smithsonian American Art Museum, Washington, DC/Art Resource, NY; pp. 8, 11 (inset), 21 © Elizabeth Larson; p. 9 Print Collection, Miriam and Ira D. Wallach Division of Art, Prints and Photographs, The New York Public Library, Astor, Lenox and Tilden Foundations; pp. 12–13 courtesy Colorado Historical Society; p. 16 courtesy Kansas State Historical Society, Hickock #10; pp. 18–19, 20 Library of Congress, Prints and Photographs Division; p. 19 (inset) Nebraska State Historical Society, RG2608; back cover © Eyewire

Library of Congress Cataloging-in-Publication Data

Dean, Arlan.
The Overland Trail : from Atchison, Kansas, to Fort Bridger, Wyoming / Arlan Dean.
   p. cm. — (Famous American trails)
Summary: Describes the Overland Trail and the frontiersmen who traveled to Fort Bridger.
Includes bibliographical references (p.) and index.
ISBN 0-8239-6479-5 (library bdg.)
1. Overland Trails—Juvenile literature. 2. Overland journeys to the Pacific—Juvenile literature. 3. Pioneers—West (U.S.)—History—19th century—Juvenile literature. 4. Frontier and pioneer life—West (U.S.)—Juvenile literature. 5. West (U.S.)—Description and travel—Juvenile literature. 6. West (U.S.)—History—1860-1890—Juvenile literature. [1. Overland Trails. 2. Overland journeys to the Pacific. 3. Pioneers. 4. Frontier and pioneer life—West (U.S.) 5. West (U.S.)—History.] I. Title.
F594 .D38 2003
978'.02—dc21

2002000150

Contents

The Overland Trail

In the 1800s, people used many different trails to travel west across America. The Overland Trail was one of the most widely used trails. This trail went from Atchison, Kansas, to Fort Bridger, Wyoming.

Check It Out

From 1862 to 1868, as many as 20,000 people used the Overland Trail each year.

The Overland Trail was made up of parts of other trails already being used. It was more than 1,100 miles long.

THE OVERLAND TRAIL

5

Dangers on the Way West

Settlers traveled west in search of a better way of life. By the 1850s, many of the trails they used were very unsafe.

Settlers traveling through the West faced the danger of attacks from Native Americans.

Native Americans often attacked settlers and people who carried mail to places in the West. The Native Americans were angry that the settlers were taking their land.

The Mail Must Get Through!

Around 1860, the United States Post Office Department hired Ben Holladay to set up a safe trail on which to take mail to the West. Holladay made the Overland Trail Mail Route. His trail passed to the south of the Oregon Trail. He tried to stay away from Native Americans who were fighting settlers.

Many Native Americans lived on the land that became the Overland Trail. They were there long before Holladay made his mail route.

In 1862, Holladay spent more than two million dollars to improve the Overland Trail and make it safe. Today, that amount would be about thirty-five million dollars!

Ben Holladay was known as the Stagecoach King because he owned so many coaches that went to the West.

Mail was carried along the Overland Trail in stagecoaches. The bags of mail were put in the back of a stagecoach.

Holladay owned the stagecoaches and mail routes on the Overland Trail.

Each mailbag weighed as much as 250 pounds. Four to six horses pulled the stagecoach.

Stagecoach

11

Life on the Trail

As many as nine people could ride inside the stagecoach. Sometimes as many as 12 people would ride on top of the stagecoach, too! The ride was very bumpy.

Tips for the Stagecoach Traveler

In 1877, the *Omaha Herald* gave travelers tips on how to act during a stagecoach trip.

"The best seat inside a stagecoach is the one next to the driver . . . you will get . . . half the bumps . . . than on any other seat."

"When the driver asks you to get off and walk, do it without grumbling."

People were thrown back and forth inside the coach. Travelers wore handkerchiefs over their noses and mouths to keep from breathing in the dust from the trail.

A crowded stagecoach

Bad weather, such as snow and hailstorms, made the trips very hard. Sometimes stagecoaches were turned over by strong winds.

"The air gets cold; the roads get dusty, and chokes . . . the legs become stiff . . . everybody is overcome with sleep, but can't stay asleep. . . ."
—From an account of an overnight coach ride, printed in a Nevada newspaper, the *Reese River Reveille,* May 1869

Sometimes a driver would lose control of the horses pulling the stagecoach. This caused the stagecoach to tip over.

Traveling by stagecoach at night was unsafe because drivers had trouble seeing the trail in the dark.

Driving a stagecoach was a job full of danger. Drivers took their coaches through narrow mountain roads. There was a chance of coaches falling down the side of the mountain. Drivers also had to watch out for attacks by robbers. Attacks by Native Americans continued to happen, too.

As a stagecoach driver, James "Wild Bill" Hickok was involved in a shoot-out with a gang of robbers.

Check It Out

James "Wild Bill" Hickok and William "Buffalo Bill" Cody were drivers for the Overland Stage Company.

William "Buffalo Bill" Cody got his nickname for providing railroad workers with buffalo meat.

Holladay set up stations, or rest stops, along the trail. There were about 80 stations between Atchison and Fort Bridger. Some stations were made with sod, chunks of dirt covered with grass. Travelers ate and slept at these stations. The food was not very good. The rooms where travelers slept were tiny and dirty.

"It was the first time we had ever seen a man's front yard on top of his house."

—Mark Twain, *on seeing a station made from dirt and grass; Twain took a stagecoach ride on the Overland Trail in 1861.*

House with a sod roof

Stagecoach station

19

The End of the Trail

The railroads came to the West in 1869. They gave people a faster and safer way to travel. The Overland Trail was no longer used as much. However, the importance of the trail was not forgotten.

The Overland Trail Time Line

1860	Ben Holladay is hired to make a safe trail west. He sets up the Overland Trail Mail Route.
1862	Holladay spends more than two million dollars to make the Overland Trail safe.
1862–1868	Over 20,000 people use the Overland Trail each year.
1869	The Overland Trail is no longer used as much because the railroads start taking people west.
2000	The Overland Trail is made an Official Millennium Trail by the U.S. government.

In 2000, the trail was made an Official Millennium Trail by the U.S. government. Today, some of the trail's stations can still be visited.

THIS MARKER ON THE
OVERLAND TRAIL.
PLATTE RIVER CROSSING
NINE MILES WEST
1861 TO 1868

ERECTED BY
THE HISTORICAL LANDMARK
COMMISSION OF WYOMING

Today, *markers show the lands that the Overland Trail crossed.*

Glossary

hailstorms (**hayl**-stormz) storms that include hail, which is small bits of ice and snow

handkerchiefs (**hang**-kuhr-chihfs) small pieces of cloth used for wiping your face or blowing your nose

Official Millennium Trail (uh-**fihsh**-uhl muh-**lehn**-ee-uhm **trayl**) a trail honored by the government for its important part in U.S. history

robbers (**rahb**-uhrz) people who steal from other people

route (**root**) a way taken to get somewhere

settlers (**seht**-luhrz) people who come to stay in a new country or place

sod (**sahd**) the top part of the soil that is covered with grass

stagecoach (**stayj**-kohch) a closed wagon pulled by horses; used for carrying people and mail, and stopped at stations for meals and fresh horses

station (**stay**-shuhn) a building built along the trail where stagecoaches stopped

Resources

Books

Children of the Trail West
by Holly Littlefield
Lerner Publishing Group (1999)

Dear Levi: Letters from the Overland Trail
by Elvira Woodruff
Random House (1997)

Web Sites

Due to the changing nature of Internet links, PowerKids
Press has developed an online list of Web sites related
to the subjects of this book. This site is updated regularly.
Please use this link to access the list:

http://www.powerkidslinks.com/fat/ovet/

Index

Word Count: 491

Note to Librarians, Teachers, and Parents

If reading is a challenge, Reading Power is a solution! Reading Power is perfect for readers who want high-interest subject matter at an accessible reading level. These fact-filled, photo-illustrated books are designed for readers who want straightforward vocabulary, engaging topics, and a manageable reading experience. With clear picture/text correspondence, leveled Reading Power books put the reader in charge. Now readers have the power to get the information they want and the skills they need in a user-friendly format.